WILD BILL
AND A BOY NAMED CHARLIE

Written by
Stephen R. Dancey

Illustrations by
Alix Mosieur

OLD MENDOTA PRESS
Mendota, Illinois.

OLD MENDOTA PRESS
A PUBLICATION COMPANY

SECOND EDITION, DECEMBER 2008

WILD BILL
AND A BOY NAMED CHARLIE

Author / Stephen R. Dancey

Illustrator / Alix Mosieur

Production Designers / James A. Harris and Philip S. Bock

Designer / David A. Bock

Editor / Cathy Bock

PRINTED IN THE UNITED STATES OF AMERICA.
ISBN   978-0-9797978-1-1

Dedicated to my grandchildren

Liam and Claire Dancey
Xander and Sam Sherman
Jillian Younger

J. B. HICKOK,
(Wild Bill.)

PREFACE

James Butler Hickok, known as Wild Bill, is one of the most famous men in the history of the Wild West. Yet much of the early writings about him were not true. This is a more accurate depiction of the gentler man who was Wild Bill.

This story is historical fiction. The events of Hickok's life are historically accurate. Charlie Black and the other characters (with the exception of the bully Jack Clark) are people listed on the Mendota, Illinois, 1870 census. The details of Hickok's visit to Mendota were included in a letter written by his mother, Polly Hickok, to his brother, Lorenzo. Henry Eby and Lucien Crooker were Civil War veterans from the Mendota area.

The photograph of Hickok wearing buckskins is probably the most familiar portrait of Hickok. Wilbur Blakeslee, a Mendota photographer, took this photograph of Wild Bill during Hickok's visit in 1869.

There is no documentation that Charlie and Hickok actually met. That part is fictional, but I tried to imagine what such a relationship may have been like, given what is known about Hickok and his personality.

Steve Dancey
August 2007
Mendota, Illinois

CHAPTER ONE

Mendota, Illinois - March, 1869

Charlie Black woke up early.

He saw the sun peeking into his window and he heard the shouts of deliverymen and the jingle of harness bells coming from the street.

Charlie had hardly slept at all. He had lain in bed eagerly waiting for morning. He sprang out of bed, threw on his clothes, and splashed some cold water on his face from the basin on the washstand.

Today was bigger than Christmas. After all, Christmas came every year; this was a once in a lifetime event. The famous lawman, scout, and adventurer Wild Bill Hickok was arriving on the train today.

"Charlie, are you up?" he heard his mother call.

"Yes, Mama, I'm ready," he called back.

Charlie ran into the kitchen. His parents had given permission for 11-year-old Charlie and his younger brother, Frank, to miss school today and accompany their father to his general store in downtown Mendota and await the arrival of the train.

Charlie frequently ran errands for his father after school. For the last week he had been hearing the men at the store talking about Hickok. Several of them even knew Hickok from childhood, and they called the famous man by his real name, James. Hickok grew up in Homer, now called Troy Grove, a small town near Charlie's hometown of Mendota, Illinois. Charlie knew his hero's full name was James Butler Hickok.

Charlie had occasionally seen Mrs. Hickok, Wild Bill's mother, in Mendota. He had even carried packages from his father's general store out to her carriage. She seemed to be a nice lady, but she wasn't different than the other ladies in town. How could she have a son like Wild Bill?

When Charlie's mother set a plate of bacon and eggs in front of him, he could hardly sit still to eat.

"What's wrong?" his mother asked, trying not to smile. "Aren't you hungry?"

"He's probably sick," teased his 15-year-old sister, Hattie. "Maybe he should just stay home today."

Charlie was irritated. "No, I'm fine. Mind your own business, Hattie. I'm going to the train station today!"

His mother smiled.

Charlie's school, Blackstone Public School in Mendota. Courtesy of the Mendota Museum & Historical Society

Alix '07

CHAPTER TWO

Charlie and Frank walked with their father to his store on Washington Street. Waiting outside the store was Frank's friend, Eddie Higgins. The train wasn't due for another hour, so the three boys walked around the block. Soon they were joined by Hiram Edwards, coming out of his father's office. Everyone in town knew Hiram's father, Dr. Joseph Edwards.

Hiram carried the February 1867 issue of Harper's New Monthly Magazine. "My father said I could have this," Hiram stated proudly. The boys studied the picture of Wild Bill Hickok on the cover and decided he looked strong and courageous.

"The article tells about a shootout Wild Bill had with David Tutt in Springfield, Missouri," Hiram said. "And it tells about the time Hickok saved the Wellmans from the McCanles Gang."

The men at the store said that Hickok had been an amazing shot, even when he was not much older than Charlie. At the age of only 13, Hickok had been hired by local farmers to track and kill a wolf! Charlie couldn't imagine doing something so brave.

The boys each shared some of the other Wild Bill Hickok stories they had heard.

After leaving Troy Grove when he was 19, Hickok had worked as a teamster and constable in Kansas. When the Civil War began, he served as a civilian scout for the Union Army. Charlie listened to the stories and was in awe of Wild Bill's bravery.

After the war ended, Hickok remained in the West and served as a scout and guide for the U.S. Cavalry. It wasn't until the Harper's article told of Hickok's many adventures that he become famous.

Charlie didn't know anyone who hadn't heard of Wild Bill Hickok. All of the boys at school dreamed of having adventures like Hickok's someday.

A short time later, Charlie and Frank ran to their father's store.

"Papa, it's time!" Frank said.

Cover of Harper's New Monthly Magazine, February, 1867. From the author's collection.

Their father smiled. "Let's close the store. No one will be shopping for a while. Everyone in town will be at the depot."

The three walked to the railroad depot where a crowd of people had gathered.

As he saw them approach, Mr. Fritz, owner of the boot store, shouted, "The train should be here soon." Mr. Fritz's three sons, Johnny, Gustave, and Frank, waved at Charlie. Charlie looked around the crowd and wondered if anyone was at school today.

It seemed like forever before Charlie heard Mr. Powell, the ticket agent, shout, "The train is coming!"

The distant roar of the train and the blowing of the whistle grew louder, and the black smoke could be seen rising over the tops of the buildings. In a short while, the train came into sight and slowed to a stop.

The conductor opened the door, and a loud cheer went up as a tall man stepped down from the passenger car. He wore a broad-brimmed hat and his light-colored hair reached past his shoulders. His eyes squinted in the bright sunlight as he gazed at the crowd.

Charlie's heart almost stopped. Hickok was finally here!

Train arriving at the depot in Mendota, Illinois. The Passenger House, a hotel where Wild Bill had a room during his visit, is the large building on the right behind the train. The Passenger House burned down in 1885. From the Leo and Norma Muhlach collection, courtesy of the Mendota Museum and Historical Society.

CHAPTER THREE

Wild Bill tipped his hat to the crowd, and everyone cheered. As Hickok walked through the crowd to the depot, Charlie noticed that he walked with a limp.

Charlie's father told the boys it was time to get back to the store. Charlie was disappointed. He had hoped that he would get to talk to Hickok.

That afternoon while Charlie and Frank were working at the store, they eagerly listened to the men talking about Wild Bill.

"William Hickok, James' father, was strongly against slavery. His house was a stop on the Underground Railroad," Mr. Higgins stated. "My uncle told me about the time James and his father went over to the Gould place one evening to pick up and hide three runaways. On their way home, they were stopped by bounty hunters looking for the slaves."

When Mr. Higgins stopped for a breath, Charlie couldn't contain himself.

"Did the bounty hunters get those poor slaves?" he asked.

"Nope," said Mr. Higgins. "Old Mr. Hickok said that James was sick with fever and pox. It was hard for the bounty hunters to see James in the dark, and I reckon they believed the story and feared they might get sick. They moved on quickly without searching the wagon. It was a close one, alright, but they were all safe."

Charlie was relieved to hear the happy ending.

Just then the door to the general store opened and in walked Wild Bill Hickok. He nodded to the men before approaching Charlie's father.

"Do you have some peaches?" Hickok asked. "I have a hankering for peaches."

"They're right over here, Mr. Hickok," said Charlie's father as he led the way. Wild Bill walked to the shelf, and Charlie again noticed that he was limping.

Hickok saw Charlie staring at his leg.

"I suppose you're wondering why I'm limping," he said.

"Well, yes," Charlie admitted timidly.

Hickok sat down on a nearby chair, stretched out his legs, and began the tale.

"I was a courier for the Cavalry. I was carrying military dispatches from Fort Wallace, Kansas, to Fort Lyon, Colorado Territory. Along the way I was attacked by a Cheyenne hunting party. One got close enough to stab me in the leg with his lance, and I barely got out with my hide," Wild Bill said.

Charlie and Frank listened quietly in amazement. Charlie imagined the terror of having to fight off Cheyenne warriors. He didn't notice that the men were just as quiet, each of them hanging on to every word.

"Well, I was alive, but my troubles weren't over. I still had a long, hard ride to the fort and my leg was hurtin' fierce. The doc at Fort Lyons fixed me as best he could. I decided to come back home and visit my family while my leg heals. I haven't seen my mother for seven years."

Hickok looked at Charlie and Frank with a twinkle in his eye. "Ma is coming to town tomorrow on the train. She's been visiting my sister, Celinda, in Malden. They're meeting me here, and I'm taking them to Troy Grove."

Hickok paused before continuing. "Boys, there is something I was wondering about. While my leg is healin', I could use someone to run errands for me. Could you boys help me out?" he asked.

"Yes, sir," Charlie said. "We'd be proud to run errands for you."

"I'm much obliged. Maybe you could help me carry these peaches back to my room," Hickok said.

Charlie quickly grabbed two cans, and Frank took another. They walked back to the Illinois Central Railroad Passenger House, where Hickok had taken a room.

"What is it like to be famous, Mr. Hickok?" Charlie asked, as they crossed Main Street.

"Well, I don't really feel famous. Most of what people write about me isn't true. Just yarns," Hickok replied. "Right now, I'm just a man anxious to see my family again."

Charlie didn't know what to say. Imagine, a gunfighter admitting he missed his family.

Photograph of Cheyenne warrior. From the author's collection.

CHAPTER FOUR

After getting back to the store, Charlie and Frank spotted Emil Haass.

"We're helping Wild Bill Hickok," they proudly told him.

Emil laughed. "Sure you are."

"We are," Frank insisted. "Wild Bill asked us to help carry his groceries, and he told us how he hurt his leg."

Charlie quickly retold the story to Emil.

Just then, Hiram Edwards ran up.

"Guess what?" he cried. "My pa is now Wild Bill Hickok's doctor. Wild Bill asked Pa to come over to the Passenger House and look at his leg."

He told the boys that his father gave Hickok some salve for his leg wound.

That evening Charlie and Frank told their mother and Hattie about their meeting with Wild Bill.

"He's not like I expected," Charlie said. "I thought he'd be mean and tough, but he talks to us like we're his friends."

"Wild Bill's mother and sister are coming in on the train from Malden tomorrow," Frank added.

The boys were at the station again the next day before the 11 a.m. train arrived.

"Oh, no," Frank said suddenly. Charlie turned around to see Jack Clark. Jack was a year older than Charlie and big for his age. He had a reputation for teasing younger children.

Jack had just tripped Johnny Fritz, who was only eight years old.

"You tripped over your own feet," Jack laughed, as Johnny blinked back tears. Charlie saw Johnny's torn pants and a little blood on his knee.

Charlie didn't even think before he spoke.

"Leave him alone!" he shouted to Jack.

"You gonna make me?" Jack asked, looking happy to have another target.

Charlie swallowed, realizing he hadn't thought this out. Jack was big and mean.

Frank tugged at his sleeve. "We better get going," he whispered to his brother.

"Are you scared?" Jack asked as he shoved Charlie.

Charlie paused before he spoke. "I don't want to fight with you. Just leave the little kids alone."

"I think you're scared," Jack jeered, pushing Charlie again.

Charlie stood his ground. "I'm not afraid of you. I just don't see any reason why there has to be trouble."

Jack's answer was a punch to Charlie's stomach. Doubled over, Charlie was afraid he might be sick. At the same time, he was angered by the sound of Jack's laughter. Charlie straightened up and swung his arm, landing a solid hit on Jack's nose.

"You'll be in big trouble for this," Jack said, wiping the blood from his nose with his sleeve. "I'm telling my father that you hit me for no reason and ruined my new shirt." Jack turned and walked away, and Charlie breathed a sigh of relief.

"Are you okay, pard'?" Charlie heard someone ask. He turned to see Hickok. "You sure took care of that bully," Hickok said with a smile.

"I'm not supposed to fight, and Mr. Clark will probably complain to my father," Charlie said glumly. "Then I'll be in trouble."

"If that happens," Hickok replied, "just let me know. I'll talk with your father. He will be proud to know how his son helped out a younger boy. I understand how you felt. The one thing I can't abide is bullies."

Charlie suddenly felt a lot better. He and Hickok had something in common.

Just then they heard the whistle and turned to watch the train as it pulled up to the depot and stopped.

Mrs. Hickok, a petite woman wearing a hat and a brown calico dress, stepped down from the train, smiled, and waved to greet her son. As she reached back to retrieve her basket, Hickok came forward, picked her up, and swung her around.

She gasped in surprise. "Oh, you never change," she laughed, hugging him. "You're still a rascal!"

"You're a sight for sore eyes, Ma," said a smiling Hickok.

Just then, a young woman stepped down from the train and ran to Wild Bill.

"James, is that really you?" she exclaimed.

"Celinda!" responded Wild Bill.

He gave his sister a hug, and the three of them were talking and smiling as they walked arm in arm towards the Passenger House.

That afternoon Hickok rented a horse and carriage from Mr. Pearson's Livery Stable on Illinois Avenue. Charlie and Frank watched them ride out of town and turn south onto the road to Troy Grove.

CHAPTER FIVE

During the next week Charlie and Frank were busy as usual. Every day after school they walked to their father's store to run errands and deliver groceries.

Mr. Black had moved Charlie's family to Mendota a few years earlier. After the construction of the Illinois Central Railroad and the Chicago, Burlington, & Quincy Railroad in the early 1850's, the town quickly sprung up where the two railroads crossed. Mendota grew into a bustling railroad town of more than 3,500 citizens.

The German and Irish immigrants who had settled in the Mendota area, as well as the many people passing through on the railroads, kept merchants, like Mr. Black, busy. There were several grocery stores, including Erlenborn's and Mr. Green's and four blacksmith shops like Mr. Kortick's and Mr. Dobbie's. Mendota even had two jewelry stores, Bush's and Pixley Brothers'.

Charlie and Frank's favorite store was Mr. Dodt's, the gunsmith's shop. The shop was near Black's General Store, and the boys walked by it on their way to and from school. They often stopped to look at the guns in the window and imagined receiving one for Christmas. That hadn't happened yet, and both boys hoped it would be this year.

Eddie Higgins and Hiram Edwards stopped by the Black's general store. Charlie and Frank's eyes grew wide when they saw what Hiram was holding—a brand new Henry Repeating Rifle! "My father gave me this for hunting," he said. It was one Charlie and Frank had admired in Mr. Dodt's window. Hiram said they were going to practice shooting and asked Charlie and Frank to come along. Eddie had a sack of empty cans to use as targets.

"Can we go, Pa?" Frank asked.

Charlie added, "We have all of our chores done."

"Well, I suppose so, but you boys be careful," Mr. Black said.

The four boys walked out of town about a mile and picked a spot just past the Castle farm. They placed five cans on the fence, and then stepped back 50 paces.

"I bet I can shoot five cans in five shots," Hiram bragged, loading a cartridge into the rifle.

After five shots, two cans were still sitting on the fence.

"That's right good shooting, but I bet I can do better than that," Eddie boasted, taking a turn with the rifle. The competition continued, and the boys pretended the cans were buffalo and outlaws.

"That's some fine shooting," a voice said from behind them. They turned and saw a smiling Hickok riding a black horse. "That looks fun. I'd like a turn." He drew his revolver, quickly rode down the line, and shot every can off the fence.

"That was great!" the boys yelled.

"Show us some more!" Charlie exclaimed.

For the next half hour, Wild Bill demonstrated his shooting skills for the boys.

"Do you think we could go out West and fight Indians and outlaws like you do?" Charlie asked.

Hickok was silent for a moment. "Well, you could," he said "but being a lawman and pistoleer is a difficult life. It's hard being alone and not knowing who you can trust. Sometimes I wish my life was more peaceful."

Charlie was surprised. He had never considered that being famous would be difficult.

Hickok continued, "I don't like violence, but I don't back down when there's trouble. Most folks don't really know me. They know the stories that have been written about me, and most of the stories aren't true."

"Well, I better be getting back home," he told the boys. "I promised my sister Celinda that I would help with some chores."

After Hickok rode off, Eddie asked the other boys, "What's a pistoleer?"

"I think it's someone who knows how to shoot quick and straight," Charlie replied.

As they walked back to town, the four boys were quiet. Finally Charlie said, "Mr. Hickok is not like I imagined. He's even better."

The other boys nodded.

CHAPTER SIX

The next week Charlie delivered a package to Hickok at the Passenger House. While he was there, Henry Eby arrived. Mr. Eby was a respected man in Mendota. He had a farm outside of town, where he lived with his wife and baby girl. He had served in the Union Army during the Civil War and had been taken prisoner by the Confederate soldiers.

"Mr. Hickok," he said, "my name is Henry Eby, and I served in the War of the Rebellion. I understand you did some scouting for us."

"Yes, sir, I did," Hickok responded, and the two men began talking.

Mr. Eby told about the sad details of battle and the miserable conditions he had endured while in Confederate prison camps.

Charlie had imagined what it was like for Mr. Eby and the other volunteers to get on the train at Mendota, bound for war. He also had imagined that the life of a soldier was filled with excitement and action. Now he knew differently.

"I'm proud to have served," Mr. Eby continued. "It was a good cause."

Hickok agreed. "Yes, we served a good cause. The slaves were freed and the Union was preserved. Sadly, though, it was a terrible loss of good men on both sides."

A few days later, the telegraph agent at the freight house, the Illinois Central Freight Depot, asked Charlie to deliver a telegram to Hickok. It was addressed to U.S. Deputy Marshal J. B. Hickok.

"Well, Charlie," Hickok said after reading the telegram, "tomorrow I'm going to Chicago for a few days. General Sheridan wants to meet with me. Senator Henry Wilson wants to take a group of important officials on a tour of the Western Territories and wants me to be their guide."

"Do you mean General Phillip Sheridan? The famous Army general?" Charlie asked.

"That's him," Hickok responded. Charlie was amazed that Hickok knew General Sheridan. Who else did Hickok know?

Henry Eby as a member of Company C, 7th Illinois Cavalry. Photograph taken in 1864. From the author's collection.

CHAPTER SEVEN

A few days later Hickok was back in Mendota. When Charlie stopped by to see if Hickok had any errands for him, he found Hickok and another man sitting on the veranda of the Passenger House. Mr. Aiken, the manager of the hotel, had placed additional benches outside so that his famous guest could sit and talk with his many visitors. Hickok had told Mr. Aiken that he preferred being outdoors.

Wild Bill invited Charlie to sit down and join him. He introduced Charlie to his brother, Horace. "We've been talking about when we were youngsters," he said.

They told Charlie a little bit about their family. Their father, William Hickok, was studying to be a Presbyterian minister when illness forced him to drop out of college. He became a merchant and then a farmer, but he remained a deeply religious man.

"Remember how Pa always had Bible verses for us to read?" Horace reminisced.

"I sure do!" Hickok answered. "He made sure each of his six children knew the Bible well. He picked out verses for me that had messages he wanted me to learn."

Charlie thought about how different this man was from the Hickok in the stories he had read.

"I remember how much you hated to do farm work," Horace said to his brother. "You were always looking for excuses to leave the farm and go hunting."

"You're right," said Wild Bill, "but you all sure enjoyed my venison and turkey. My hunting and tracking skills continue to serve me well."

"When we were children I enjoyed the yarns you told to amuse us. And then you grew up to have adventures just like those tales you told," Horace said with a smile.

Hickok laughed. "I had fun entertaining you with my stories."

Charlie enjoyed listening to the conversation between Horace and Wild Bill. He wished he could stay longer, but he knew it was time to go. "I have to get back to the store," he said reluctantly. "My father said not to be gone long."

"It was good to meet you, Charlie," said Horace. "Maybe I'll see you again. I'll be back to visit this guy soon, just to make sure he stays out of trouble."

"Now, Horace, since when could you keep me out of trouble?" joked Wild Bill.

As Charlie walked back to the store, he heard Wild Bill and his brother laughing. It had been a good afternoon.

Left to Right: Horace Hickok, Capt. Jack Crawford, (a friend of Wild Bill) and Dr. Joseph Edwards, Hiram's father, taken at Troy Grove, Illinois in 1916. From the Leo and Norma Muhlach collection, courtesy of the Mendota Museum and Historical Society.

CHAPTER EIGHT

Hickok spent most of his days walking around Mendota and talking with the townspeople. When his leg began to hurt, he would sit outside the Passenger House, and the people would come there to talk with him.

Charlie stopped by the Passenger House one day to find Hickok cleaning his Colt Navy revolvers.

"Why do you carry two guns?" Charlie asked.

"Because sometimes they misfire," Hickok explained. "These Colts are very accurate, and I consider them the best guns made. But, as you know, if the gunpowder gets a little damp, the gun misfires. I can't risk having a misfire, so I carry two guns."

A voice from behind said, "Hello there, Mr. Hickok."

Charlie and Hickok turned as two men approached. The older man spoke. "I'm Lucien Crooker. I have a law practice here in Mendota and currently serve as the city attorney. A friend of mine, Henry Eby, said he met you last week. We both served in the War of the Rebellion, and I know you helped us out quite a bit," Crooker said.

Hickok stood and shook Crooker's hand. "Pleased to make your acquaintance," Hickok said.

The second man also held out his hand for Hickok's handshake. "I'm Robert Ruggles. I own The Bulletin, Mendota's newspaper. I'd like to interview you for the paper. Our readers are very interested in your adventures."

Hickok was silent for a minute.

"I don't know," replied Hickok. "Many of the things written about me aren't true and are not what I want my mother to read."

"Here at The Bulletin, we strive for accuracy," Mr. Ruggles assured him.

Captain Lucien B. Crooker of Company F
55th Illinois Infantry.

Photograph taken in 1863. From the
author's collection.

View of Mendota, Illinois, 1869. The large building in the center is the Passenger House where Wild Bill stayed during his visit. The building in front to the right is the Illinois Central Freight Depot. From the Leo and Norma Muhlach collection, courtesy of the Mendota Museum and Historical Society.

"Well, then I reckon it's all right," Hickok agreed. "As you probably know, I left Troy Grove in 1856 and headed to Kansas with my older brother, Lorenzo. When Lorenzo came back home, I stayed with the Cody family. You may have heard of their son, William. Now he's called Buffalo Bill."

Charlie listened to every word. He was astonished that Hickok knew Buffalo Bill!

Lorenzo Butler Hickok, Wild Bill's older brother. Photograph taken in 1864. Courtesy of the Mendota Museum and Historical Society.

Wild Bill continued. "Then I went to Monticello, Kansas, and worked as a constable. I don't mind telling you, Kansas is a rough place, and it wasn't easy trying to maintain law and order. I guess that's where I got the reputation as a gunfighter, but I was only doing my job. Later, I worked as a teamster, driving freight wagons."

"When the War of the Rebellion broke out, I offered my services as a civilian scout for the Union Army. My father had taught me slavery was wrong, and I was proud to serve.

"After the war, I worked as a government detective for the Army, tracking down deserters and also retrieving stolen military property. Then I was a guide and scout for Lieutenant Colonel George Armstrong Custer and the Seventh Cavalry. I'm sure you've heard of Custer. He became well-known during the War."

Charlie was thrilled that Hickok knew Custer!

Hickok paused for a minute and then continued. "A few years ago I met George Nichols, a writer for Harper's Magazine. He had heard about me and asked me to tell about some of my adventures. Well, I'm sorry to say I exaggerated a little, and he exaggerated a little more when he wrote the article. What was printed just wasn't accurate. People believed what they read, and when they retold the stories, the tall tales got even taller."

"Anyway, in 1867 I was appointed Deputy U.S. Marshal in Kansas. Last month, I was scouting for the cavalry, when I was wounded. It was then that I decided to come back to visit my family."

"Well, Mr. Hickok, you've certainly lead an exciting life," Mr. Ruggles said. "I don't think we'll need any exaggerations to keep our readers interested. The truth is interesting enough."

The men all shook hands, and the visitors left.

"I sure hope that Mr. Ruggles keeps his word," Hickok told Charlie.

"Don't worry," Charlie assured him. "My father said Mr. Ruggles is an honest man."

Hickok adjusted the revolvers on his belt. "I'll walk back to the store with you, Charlie," he said. "I'm headin' to Mr. Blakeslee's studio now. I promised my mother I'd have my photograph taken while I was home."

Charlie and Hickok walked together to Mr. Black's General Store before Hickok continued on to the Blakeslee Studio.

Photograph of Wild Bill Hickok taken at the Blakeslee Studio in Mendota, Illinois in 1869. Courtesy of the Kansas State Historical Society.

CHAPTER NINE

Hickok had been in the Mendota area for nearly two months, and Charlie had become accustomed to stopping by the Passenger House after school each day. He began to think Hickok might be staying permanently.

But one day when he arrived, Hickok had some news for Charlie.

"Charlie," Hickok said, "I reckon it's time to say good-bye. You've been a good friend these past weeks. My leg is healed now, and it's time for me to get back to Kansas. I'm leaving for Hays City on tomorrow's train."

"Already?" Charlie asked. "Can't you stay longer?"

Hickok laughed. "If I stay much longer, people will be tired of me and run me out of town."

"C'mon, no one could ever get tired of seeing you around. You're the most exciting person ever to come to Mendota," Charlie said with conviction. "When I grow up I want to go out West and be a teamster or a scout for the Army or maybe a lawman, just like you."

"I'm proud that you want to be like me," Hickok told him, "but follow your own trail and see where it leads you.

"You've been a good pard'," Hickok said to Charlie. "I have something special I want to give you." Hickok handed him a beaded sheath and knife.

 "Is this a real Indian knife?" Charlie asked breathlessly.

"It sure is. It belonged to a Cheyenne warrior. I got it while I was scouting for Custer and the Seventh Cavalry."

"Thank you, Mr. Hickok!" Charlie exclaimed. "This is the best gift ever."

"Well, I'll ask just one favor in return," Hickok said. "Don't believe everything you read about me."

"Oh, I won't, Mr. Hickok," Charlie answered.

"Watch your topknot, pard'," Hickok said with a smile. "Stand tall, Charlie. A hero is someone who protects what is right and good. Do that, and you'll be a hero too."

Hickok tipped his hat, and Charlie watched him walk slowly toward the Passenger House for the final time. Once more Charlie was in awe of this peaceful man called Wild Bill.

AFTERWORD

James Butler Hickok left Mendota, Illinois, in May 1869 and never returned. His adventures in the West continued. He served as sheriff of Ellis County, Kansas, and later as Marshall of Abilene, Kansas.

On August 2, 1876 Wild Bill Hickok was shot and killed while playing poker in Deadwood, Dakota Territory. He was widely respected as a lawman, and his legend continues even today.

Charlie grew up to be a businessman and was a hero to his family and friends.

James Butler "Wild Bill" Hickok

Born May 27, 1837 in Homer, Illinois
(present-day Troy Grove)

Killed August 2, 1876 in Deadwood,
Dakota Territory.

*"Whenever you get into a row be sure and not
shoot too quick. Take time. I've known many
a feller to slip up for shootin' in a hurry."*

Wild Bill Hickok — *Harpers New Monthly
Magazine,* Februrary, 1867.

AN EYEWITNESS ACCOUNT

Anna Wilson Herrick moved to Mendota, Illinois with her parents in March of 1856 when she was two months old.

In August 1953 during Mendota's Centennial Celebration, 97-year-old Anna Wilson Herrick was interviewed about Mendota's early history. Anna gave the following account during the interview.

One warm April day in 1869, thirteen-year-old Anna and her mother were walking along Washington Street in Mendota. They approached a group of men standing and talking at the corner of Main Street and Washington Street near Black's General Store. Anna's mother identified the tall man standing in the center of the group as the famous scout and lawman James Hickok.

As they passed by the men, Anna says she looked up and smiled at Mr. Hickok, and he smiled back at her and tipped his wide-brimmed hat.

Washington Street, Mendota, Illinois at the time of Wild Bill Hickok. The building at the end of the street on the far right is Black's General Store. The building at the end of the street on the left, with the long roof, is the Illinois Central Freight Depot. The depot is still there today. From the Leo and Norma Muhlach collection, courtesy of the Mendota Museum and Historical Society.

A MYSTERY SOLVED

One of the most famous photographs of Wild Bill Hickok is a full-figure standing image of him wearing buckskins. The original photograph is a *carte de visite,* also known as a CDV. A *carte de visite,* first introduced in 1854, is an albumen print mounted on a 2 ½ " by 4" card. The imprint on the back of the card of the Hickok photograph identifies Wilbur Blakeslee as the photographer and gives the location of his Mendota, Illinois studio.

Some historians still questioned whether or not the photograph was actually taken in Mendota by Blakeslee. Nineteenth century photographers often copied each other's photographs and sold them as their own by remounting them on a different card and imprinting their name on the back.

In April 2005 an important old photograph album was discovered in an antique shop. Stephen Dancey found that the album contained several CDV images with Wilbur Blakeslee's name and the location of his Mendota studio imprinted on the back. All the photographs were circa 1868–1869 and are unknown family photographs not worthy of being pirated by another 19th century photographer to claim as his own.

Two photographs in the album very clearly show that the distinctive pattern of the carpet in the Blakeslee studio matches the pattern of the carpet in the photograph of Hickok. We now know for sure that the famous photograph of Wild Bill in buckskins was taken by Wilbur Blakeslee in his Mendota, Illinois studio during Wild Bill Hickok's historic 1869 visit.

Compare the pattern of the carpet in the photograph above with the photograph on the opposite page that is known to have been taken at the Blakeslee Studio. Courtesy of the Kansas State Historical Society.

The pattern of the carpet in this photograph, known to have been taken at the Blakeslee Studio in Mendota, Illinois, is identical to the photograph on the opposite page. This provides clear evidence that the photograph of Wild Bill Hickok was also taken at the Blakeslee Studio. From the author's collection.

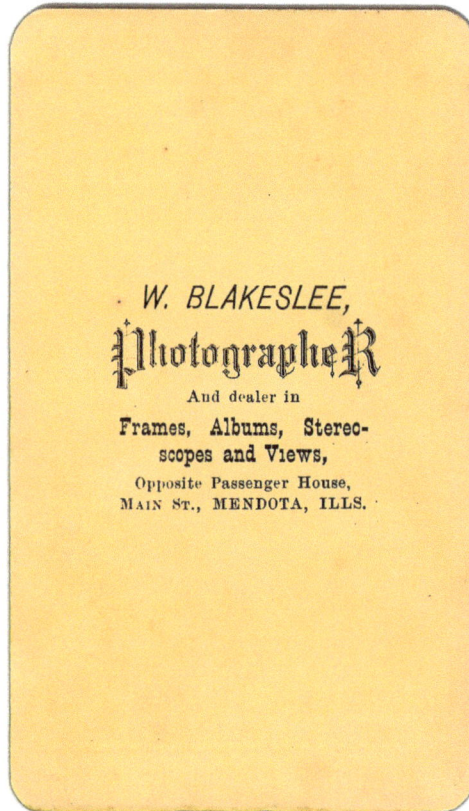

Above: Sample imprint from the Blakeslee Studio printed on the reverse side of a *carte de visite* photograph, actual size. From the author's collection.

Opposite page: Wild Bill Hickok. From the Leo and Norma Muhlach collection, courtesy of the Mendota Museum and Historical Society.

ABOUT THE AUTHOR

Stephen R. Dancey is a Retired Master Sergeant with the Illinois State Police. During his career Steve was Field Training Officer Supervisor, Officer in Charge of the Tactical Response Team and Weapons Instructor for ISP District 2, Elgin, Illinois. He was also an Instructor at the Illinois State Police Academy in Springfield, Illinois.

Currently Steve is a Historian and Story Teller for the Mendota Museum and Historical Society in LaSalle County, Illinois.

One of the highlights of Steve's career as a historian was time spent in two summer seasons as an interpreter at the Little Big Horn Battlefield National Monument in Montana. Steve was especially privileged to have also spent several weeks in study at the Pine Ridge Sioux Reservation in South Dakota.

Steve is a life-long Wild Bill Hickok enthusiast and has given several lectures on the life and times of Wild Bill. This book is a dream fulfilled.

Steve lives in Mendota, Illinois with his wife Carole. While continuing to work on several historical projects, both he and Carole are active in the community.

www.ingramcontent.com/pod-product-compliance
Lightning Source LLC
LaVergne TN
LVHW072107070426
835509LV00002B/59